WHAT THE LIVING WON'T LET GO

BOOKS BY LORNA CROZIER

Inside Is the Sky 1976
Crow's Black Joy 1979
Humans and Other Beasts 1980
No Longer Two People (with Patrick Lane) 1981
The Weather 1983
The Garden Going On Without Us 1985
Angels of Flesh, Angels of Silence 1988
Inventing the Hawk 1992
Everything Arrives at the Light 1995
A Saving Grace 1996
What the Living Won't Let Go 1999

What the Living
Won't Let Go

LORNA CROZIER

M&S

Canadian Cataloguing in Publication Data

Crozier, Lorna, 1948-
What the living won't let go

Poems.
ISBN 0-7710-2481-9

I. Title.

PS8555.R72W42   1999   C811'.54   C98-932935-6
PR9199.3.C66W42   1999

We acknowledge the financial support of the Government of Canada
through the Book Publishing Industry Development Program
for our publishing activities. We further acknowledge the support
of the Canada Council for the Arts and the Ontario Arts Council
for our publishing program.

Typeset in Garamond by M&S, Toronto
Printed and bound in Canada

McClelland & Stewart Inc.
The Canadian Publishers
481 University Avenue
Toronto, Ontario
M5G 2E9

I 2 3 4 5   03 02 01 00 99

For my brother, Barry, and my companion, Patrick,
with love and admiration.

CONTENTS

I

Names of Loss and Beauty

NAMES OF LOSS AND BEAUTY

I've never seen a catalpa tree
or one that bears persimmons.
Since moving to the Coast
I've noted others on the calendar,
their blossoming time: magnolia, dogwood,
and a bush called piers japonica.
In May wisteria tumbles from our roof
as if rain thought itself inside
a flower, another way of falling.
I don't know what this new beauty means.
I've lost so many things
I once thought dear and permanent.
A few good friends, the blue
snow gives back to morning.
I could list more here, but what's the sense?
Magnolia petals shine so much like flesh
without the stains or softness
aging brings,
it hurts to watch them fall.

Waiting six years
since my brother drifted from my touch.
I have almost forgotten his smell,
forgotten how we moved together,
water over water, breath riding breath
into the emptiness of blue.

It is the night of my arrival.
My father sits on the couch,
throws a ball for the bull terrier
they've called Patsy.
Behind him my mother bends,
unfastens her stockings.
They slide down her legs
with the sound of sunlight
slipping through the petal of a peony.
Soon he will turn to her.

These are the two
I love and will love
no matter what they do to me
or to each other.
This is my brother's house.

He has opened a window in his room,
the night hot and sticky.
He is trying not to hear

through the wall that keeps him
from the huge bed
they won't let him sleep in any more.

Lightly as a moth I slip
through the screen. He feels
a breeze lifting his hair.
It is me, breathing over him,
savouring his smell,
dusting my small hands
across his forehead
till my mother cries that cry
and I must go.

Months later when he leans
over my crib
he will see it in my eyes,
the way I look at him
as if I know
what he's forgotten

and the first
of the many times
he'll deny me
will begin.

COYOTE HOUNDS

They're thin. A shadow of the wind
the windmill flattens in the grass.
My uncle keeps them in back of the barn,
feeds them bones with little meat upon them.
They growl and tear. Sometimes for hours
they stare at the cow's fat udder, her rich
brown moons of shit. There is straw
to sleep on. It smells of mice and crickets,
dust and sun. It smells of the pigskin gloves
my uncle wears when he comes for them.

Sometimes I look in. Something about me
turns them fierce and raucous. "Good dog,"
I say, "good boy," meaning all of them.
They'd show me their bellies if I dared
come near. He is the only one
who touches them, throws them in the truck
if they're slow, cuffs them if they cower.
Then there's the ride across pastures
at dusk or early morning, wind slicking
the hair along their backs, rare licks of rain.

Later, they clean the blood from their muzzles.
In the narrow darkness of their stall
they crack the marrow bones and circle sleep.
It is then I move inside their dream,
stroke the russet foreheads,

pull out thorns of prickly pears.
To them my scent is strong
as coyote's and more strange.

They love the chase, the smell the coyote's paws
scatter on the trail like bits of rotting meat,
the smell that streams in radiant ribbons
from his fur. Oh, you should hear them then!
They have big chests and hearts.
They howl their hunger for this wild
brother some call the Dog of God.
He is not. He's them without a master,
without a cage. Don't pity him.
Every night he eats the moon.

I died, once, in the water.
I could hear my father's boat
till he cut the motor,
then I saw its shadow large and flat –
a manta ray above my head –
a strange drumming all around me.

Everything was loud –
sound and echo inseparable.
They met where I hung suspended.

My father pounded the side of the boat
with the heels of his hands,
cast lures baited with his flesh,
a spur of bone.

There was a point where light
no longer reached me.
Mouths, muscular and cold,
bumped my legs, something
ran its beak down my vertebrae
like a stick striking pickets.

When I rose, eyes wide open,
water poured from my nose and mouth,
my bones ran liquid.
It was the same inside and out.

I drifted in bed for days,
my heart another drumming,
its rivers cold as water
from the bottom of the sea.
Every morning it seemed to be raining;
fish flared and glided on the ceiling
in constant streams of light.

Even in dreams I heard
my father weeping,
his body dark and grieving.
Across the blankets fell the shadow
I knew I must kick towards
to live. It did not feel
like being born again.

WE CAME INTO THE NIGHT, SINGING

That winter we were ten, her voice
so lovely I thought it mine,
I sang loud with everything I had
till the teacher put me in the back
with the tone-deaf boys
told to mouth the words.

Dark at 4 p.m., we slid on ice
down the hill from school.
In her room we made up stories
of what we thought was love,
touched ourselves and then each other,
felt something we couldn't speak
though there was pleasure in it,
and fear, and every night in bed
I prayed I'd stop. All that season

between school and home
streetlights shot radiant columns
from the toes of our boots
into the sky. It was the first I knew
I had a soul. Worried by wind,
snow in the beams rose and fell at once.

It climbed high enough to see
beyond the shimmer where night
held our childhood like a glass globe

turned upside down then righted,
everything inside it
there to catch the glitter –
the evergreen, the little house,
the deer that never moved.

On the street with my friend
I threw my body into song,
the grace notes of a girl
told she couldn't stay in key.
Far from our mothers
I moved my lips to her voice
and we kissed each other
as snow, mouthing the words,
fell into the silences we made.

THE NIGHT OF MY CONCEPTION 2

Mist in the fields. Inside it,
a rabbit and a wishing stone.

A man and woman lie in their own
whiteness, the brief balsam of the flesh.

Her hair is darker than I've seen it,
his less thin. When I look closer

the mist thickens, but I glimpse
the round gleam of his buttocks

and one of her breasts, from under him,
fallen a little to the side.

Its nipple is a rose quartz
polished by his tongue,

a stone for several wishes.
I am less corporeal than water,

than the rabbit, smaller
than a child's footprint on a page.

Soon the man and woman will make
a space for me between them.

Sweet Jesus, he cries,
and I'm the one who answers.

Smaller than a barley pearl,
I curl inside her longing.

It is my voice
singing when she comes.

PLAYING DEAD

Eyes closed tight as fists
clutching stones, the child
feels each of the red ant's feet
as it climbs her knee.

Wind ruffles the grass
the way her hand strokes
the bristles on her mother's brush
until they spark and snap.
A shadow ripples across her face,
something between her body
and the sun. *You can't get me,*
she wants to whisper. *I'm dead.*

The shadow makes her shiver.
She seems to be falling into it
as you'd fall through ice,
the hard light breaking.

I've tricked you, she tries to say,
I'm only playing *dead.*

She waits for laughter.
She waits for someone
to pinch and make her squeal.

Where is her mother?
Why isn't her mother holding her close,
brushing and brushing the cold
from her hair until it gleams.

THOMAS HARDY'S HEART

My name is Jude. I am the cat who swallowed
Thomas Hardy's heart. I snatched it
from the bowl in my mistress's kitchen
and leapt through the window to the woods.

She was his sister.
What was she going to do with it?
Stuff it with veal and breadcrumbs?
Soak it in cider and serve it with the funeral meats?

It pumped a trail across the sill
and then the paving stones,
pounding out its life. I believe
she'll never get over it,
such screams and shrieking, her face
drunk with tears.

Plump as a rat and slippery,
he would have said *the deadest thing*
– it was the strangest thing
I've ever eaten. In the mouth it was sweet;
in the belly, all wormwood and rue.

Better than a tongue, a bitter heart
speaks truly. I had nine lives.
Now I've ten.

At night my mistress walks the woods,
bare trees flecked with candlelight,
a pulse that flickers in her hand.
Twice no one dies.
I've eaten nothing since.

In a plaintive voice she calls.
First *Jude*, then *Thomas*, then *Jude* again.
The warmth of her lap, the nest I made
from her hair spread across the pillow
like a pelt, no muscle underneath
so it was also a darkling stream.

What dreams I've had!
My hands are paws.
Was she the one who used to feed me
when I was young?

The sky is clear tonight –
out of the woods I don't know what to come to
or if I should at all

starlit in my loneliness and magic in my eyes.

VISIT

Tonight my father's at the door.
In the wedding suit he's grown big
enough to fit again. I've seen it only
in the dust-bowl picture by Mom's bed.

What do you want? I ask as if he's here
to sell me something or save my soul.
I have my own religion. I don't mean
to be rude. It's just the shock – my father
in the porchlight, mute, his wedding suit.

You'd think he'd speak.
Six years since the tumours
closed his throat. Maybe death
leaves us our afflictions –
they're what the living won't let go.

I do my best not to picture him in bed,
that thick gargle in his throat,
milk pouring from his nose.
What do you want to say?

Before my eyes, he grows thin again,
his jacket merely cloth without the breadth
to make it him, standing there in front of me,
so many moths stuttering from the gabardine
they dust the light until the light goes out.

THE SPIRIT FOX

The cattle of the spirit move slowly
along the borders of your sleep,
dark behemoths of warmth, valleys
of their backs and shoulders
damp with dew.

Then there is the spirit fox,
red and lean as fire turned into muscle.

The cattle are always there, just
beyond your dreams, your body
heavy with the thought of them,
but you see the fox only
in the way you see your breath
on a cold clear day,
that surprise of the invisible
where your mouth meets the air.

The cattle graze in winter pastures,
look up with great calm eyes
as if they do not know you,
as if you make no difference.

Their insouciance, the soothing bigness
of the hips and udders of the cows
startles you
as if it all comes down to birth.

Paws hushed by snow,
by prairie wool, the fox
steps just behind you. You feel
its gaze on the back of your neck

and you're afraid to turn
into the green flint of its stare
you know will see too much of you
and leave nothing out.

THE SOUNDS A WOMAN MAKES

He parks the car down the block
and walks through darkness to the house.
On his neighbour's porch two pumpkins
sink into softness, their grins collapsed.
A familiar truck sits in his driveway
like a stray dog that won't go away,
him asking, *Do we want this?*
his wife scraping leftovers into a bowl
and placing it outside.

It's been one of those strange Octobers
that bite into summer and won't let go,
alleys stinking with heat. He hears
a raccoon back of the house,
picking through garbage.
Though his own face and head are bare
he feels tonight as if he too
wears a darkness around his eyes.

At the side of the house
he stands under the upstairs window.
Like the warm breath of an animal
a breeze nuzzles his neck,
rises and sighs through the screen.
Against the porch four storm windows lean.

[handwritten annotation in right margin:] orange October / nights / blue black / concerns of / darkness.

It seems harder every fall
to climb the ladder with that weight,
lug the panes, rung by rung,
without losing his footing or breaking
the glass. He looks up as if that's what
he's planning. Above, through the screen,
he hears her cry.

Even as a child, he had a good sense of timing.
Skimming the ice, his feet on blades
slashed ahead so he'd be where the puck
would meet the wood, that hard thwack
shuddering up the stick to his shoulder blades,
reverberating through his bones
like the sounds a woman makes.

My little howler monkey, he used to tease,
my moon wolf.

In the odd October heat, the flames
of aspen leaves hurt the night.
They reach through his eyes
and burn inside though it isn't anger
he's feeling now, it isn't pain.

When she stops,
he knows all that he was
has been whittled away.

Below their bedroom window
he stands in the beauty of new wood,
naked and gleaming,
before it can be made into anything
a man might use.

The summer of the large hats,
one loud with sunflowers, three of them
rustling around the brim, the other with
a big red rose woven wonderfully from wicker.
We were women with good hair and wore hats
rarely. Hers fell blonde and thick
straight to her shoulders like water
through a sieve. You could see
the line where the scissors had cut.
Mine was chestnut, naturally curly,
more abundant when the air was damp.

We were like two fillies glimpsed in a field
as you drive past, one palomino,
one sorrel, needing nothing but the grass,
wind running like a boy between us in the sun.
Left on our own too much, she'd say later.

I taught her how to catch tree frogs,
dusty green, so many that summer in the grass.
I'd cup my hand where I thought they'd land –
they'd leap and I'd scoop them up. How sweet
to hold one in my palm and stroke its back
freckled like her shoulders in her red dress.
I could hardly let them go.

At night we tucked my daughter, her small son,
in rollaways on the porch.
We sipped wine that tasted of oak from the cask
and had that colour to it. Her skin, too,
bathed in lamplight. Any moment
our husbands would arrive from the city.
We'd wear our hats for them.

As moths with silver wings
dusted their desire across the screens
our hands cast rabbit, antelope, and mare
on whitewashed walls. Her fingers
ran down my belly like a mouse.

The third Friday I told my husband not to come,
said I was sick of the country
and would be with him in a day or two.
Though we'd agreed, she didn't make her call.
That weekend she was quiet
but I heard her husband through the wall –
it was like putting my hand in fire,
holding it there.

That last afternoon, away from him
we picked saskatoons in the coulee's dip,
our mouths purpling the skin
under each other's blouse as if a button had been
pressed too hard. The first piece is for you,
she said, when the pie turned out golden.

In front of him I took a bite, spat it out.
She'd mistaken the crystals in their pantry jar
– the pie was full of salt. He laughed too loud
as if he knew everything.

The hat with the rose hung on a hook
by my bedroom mirror for years
till my daughter took it down, needing
the costume of a lady for the school play.
I've never loved myself so much.

                    That summer,
berries exploded on the stems,
wild canaries carried her blondeness
from my fingers to the trees, brightening
everything they touched, my mouth
salty with the taste of her.

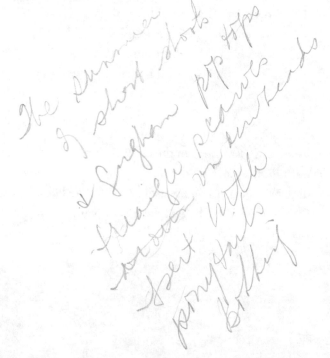

If my friend hadn't loved
the mole on the side of my right foot –
a beauty mark, she said –
would I have noticed when it twinned
to twice its size? A perfect heart
some child had cut from folded paper
then opened it and spread it flat.

Melanoma.

When I say the word out loud
vowels unfurl off my tongue,
petals on a flower I've never seen before –
mimosa, bougainvillaea. May 24, 1948,
the gardener's youngest daughter writes,
The melanoma blooms so lush this year
bees wake us every morning.

A wild sea shipwrecks me on Maui,
Bali, Melanoma – the lost misty isle
where the last of the lepers live.
Shy and ancient, one stares at me
with half a face through thick wet leaves.

Rare spices of the East –
melanoma, tamarind, cardamom –

worth their weight in gold.
A little goes a long way.

Melanoma, first name Carmen,
the famous middle-aged flamenco dancer
García Lorca applauded in Granada.
Five o'clock in the afternoon
in saffron candlelight
he could hear *duende*
in the pounding of her heels.

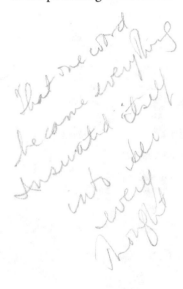

MILDRED

The panties I buy wear a sticker:
Inspected by Mildred.
All the pairs in my drawer
have passed through her hands
before I slip them on.

I've been buying this brand
for years because of Mildred.
What kind of trouble can I get into
wearing panties inspected
by Mildred? How can I not
keep my knees together, my
underwear clean?

The elastic still snaps
after countless washes,
the seams hold, the 100% cotton
hugs the hips and bum
because my panties have been
inspected by Mildred.

What will I do when she retires?
When her name is replaced
by Tonya or Charlotte,
someone who wears silk and lace
or nothing at all, someone who
doesn't know the first thing

about the tenacity of
the double-lined
cotton crotch?

I hope Mildred has medicare,
a dental plan, and wages
that match her labour.
I hope she works
in a factory full of windows,
in a comfortable chair,
pulling panties over her hands
like evening gloves and holding them
to the light with the close attention
of a woman candling eggs.

Hail to thee, sweet Mildred,
Mother of Cotton Panties,
immaculate and flawless,
for the blossoms of your labour,
for the blessings of your hands.

Something always happens here,
the waitress says. Yesterday
a woman hit her husband with her purse.
He threw it in the fountain – lipstick,
tampons, comb floating like those little boats
children sail on holidays.

Today there is a man, a gypsy, I am told,
in a torn T-shirt, three words glittering
across his back: *Inspire, Admire, Expire.*
Beside the tables where students chat
and touch each other
he sips from a bottle, holds a small torch
to his lips and breathes.
A whoosh of fire explodes in the wind,
his dark face lit. When we applaud he grins,
the lines in his face traced with soot.
It's easy to believe this is the only thing
he knows.

In boots and tight red jeans
he struts across the square, spits flames
at the fountain like a fireman in reverse.
I drop ten francs into his cap.
Too much, the waitress says
in the voice the young reserve
for the demented and the old.

He'll think he's got the best of you.
She tells me he won't leave now till I go.

His dark eyes dart among the tables
like city sparrows after crumbs. Something
always happens here. What about the woman
who hit her husband with her purse?
If she had seen this man breathe fire
would he have got the best of her?

The students turn away from him
back to one another, their laughter
a clatter of cups and spoons.
I'd like to tell the waitress
I've not given him enough, imagine
his tongue on me, the danger as it flicks
from breast to thigh. I want to know
what it is he knows,
the lies fire's taught him –
words that chafe the mouth with kisses
and taste of light.

THE WILD SWANS OF BLED
(Yugoslavia, 1989)

Beaks tucked into wings, necks resting
along their backs, they floated past,
the only brightness on the lake at Bled.
Headless, they'd lost the shape of birds,
instead were boats
folded from the finest paper
or feathered baskets full of souls.

Alone in the dark she and her brother
stood together in the wonder of it,
her hand in his. Far from friends
he was not ashamed of her awkward
adoration, he, all she knew of love
before she knew a man.

This was to be their last vacation,
their last hotel. They'd slipped through shadows
in the lounge past their parents drinking
slivovitz more colourless than laughter
with the joy gone out of it. Hardly
children then, but they should have been
in bed, warm under eiderdown,
snow falling as it does in dreams
high in the mountains.

Swans, her brother said and called them
Mute, his voice clear
as the first words ever spoken.

Then the moon appeared
and they were brighter, candlelit.
Small white coffins, she said, *for babies
smothered in their beds.*
He laughed and dropped her hand,
stepped into the dark that made
another lake behind her in the grass.
Did she imagine wings then
lifting out of sleep to touch her hair,
above the water necks waving
through the air like wands?

Neither of them knew
he would be gone within the year,
their country ripped apart
as easily as feathered breasts
are split in two.
She will not think of him
as he is now.

If he could say one word to her
would it be *swan*? Five –
or were there seven sleeping on the lake,
she and he both knowing
there was something they should do.

They couldn't have flown.
Should they have stayed there in the night,
drifted in that long, deep dreaming?

So white and silent, yet there seemed to be
a sound there too –
the whoosh of snow caving in a wall
in a city one of them would know
too soon, the exhalation of a body
as it falls.

Take the thickest socks.
Wherever you're going
you'll have to walk.

There may be water.
There may be stones.
There may be high places
you cannot go without
the hope socks bring you,
the way they hold you
to the earth.

At least one pair must be new,
must be blue as a wish
hand-knit by your mother
in her sleep.

*

Take a leather satchel,
a velvet bag and an old tin box –
a salamander painted on the lid.

This is to carry that small thing
you cannot leave. Perhaps the key
you've kept though it doesn't fit
any lock you know,

the photograph that keeps you sane,
a ball of string to lead you out
though you can't walk back
into that light.

In your bag leave room for sadness,
leave room for another language.

There may be doors nailed shut.
There may be painted windows.
There may be signs that warn you
to be gone. Take the dream
you've been having since
you were a child, the one
with open fields and the wind
sounding.

*

Mistrust no one who offers you
water from a well, a songbird's feather,
something that's been mended twice.
Always travel lighter
than the heart.

2

Counting the Distance: Another Family's Story

THE YOUNGER SISTER: WEATHER WATCH

She'd brood in weather of her own making.
My sister and I'd watch through the window
as she paced in the yard. Impossible
to read the flush she wore those days
like a hunger she couldn't bear
as if we'd emptied all her cupboards
and licked the bowls clean.

It had something to do with our father
gone again, something to do with what
we would become. We'd watch
and wait, counting the distance
between light and thunder
until there was no number
small enough to measure.

The sky's bruise built in the heat
beyond some breaking point,
those nights she brought the weather in,
its flash floods, its uprootings,
and after, in the silence that followed

all our weeping, one of us would hold her,
the other assess the damage,
calculate the cost – what could be
healed or mended, what pains we could take

to keep us whole and loving,
her power spent, the sky now burning
clear then golden, holding in its arms
all it had to give us, after rain.

THE YOUNGER SISTER: TOO CLOSE TO THINGS

My sister's breasts were shy as fawns
and like a fawn they hushed you
when you glimpsed their sheen,
filled you with tenderness and wonder –
you had to touch them. We shared
the bath until her legs grew long,
her beauty made me stare. In spring
thick with run-off the creek bent
towards her, the willow in the yard
let down its hair to hide her from the sun.
Only she could calm our mother, her blue
eyes soothed as water smooths a stone.

Once, I saw her with a fox
in the coulee at the edge of town,
I'd swear she held its paw
and when she turned to look at me
her eyes flashed green. Sage
and mother's camphor were her smells.
They left a spoor the boys would follow,
startling her at night, their eyes
upon her – motionless –
as if they held her in a rifle scope,
trigger fingers taut, love too soft
a word for what they felt. Mornings
on the path below our window
I'd find some boy's silver slick

like the trail a snail will leave
in its slow slide across the grass.

The crow who woke us long before the light
left my sister gifts in the birdbath –
once, a sparrow's wing, a heron's foot,
the velvet body of a mole. Even then
I knew she came too close to things.
Nothing I could do would make her stop.

THE OLDER SISTER: HUNTER'S MOON

In the fall, red leaves
splattered the ground, the moon
bloody too, our father would return,
deer or antelope spread-eagled
on the car roof, its stare
the deadest thing I'd seen.
I disappeared while he sawed
and wrapped the flesh,
buried the head without its rack
behind the burning barrel.

It is said if you kill a buck
his wife will seduce you,
lead you through the grasslands
till you are lost. That fall
our father was distracted.
His gaze moved far beyond
what we could see, hills yellow
in the last of heat, silver where
wolf willow hugged the rills.

Our mother simpered at the table,
dipped her tongue in sugar.
Jumping up and down
she filled his plate till food
spilled over on the cloth.

Every afternoon she changed
into something finer, practised smiling
in the mirror above the kitchen sink.
She licked her lips so often
it became a habit she couldn't break.
His tires spitting gravel, she stood
at the window, the stiffness of new cotton
against her skin finally loosening
in the breeze that accompanies
the sun going down.

The antelope wife, her two daughters,
waited in the dusk, first frost
feathering the grass. Offering him
an easy silence we couldn't give
they led him through the hills,
the season of the trembling aspen,
our father lost forever from our lives.

THE BOY: THE ONLY WAY TO EXPLAIN IT

Our spaniel in heat,
Dad locked her in the shed.
He wanted purebred pups. He'd pay
a stud fee and make 200 bucks
a litter. In the middle of the night
the neighbour's lab
crashed through the window.
Head bloody, he humped our bitch.
Dad couldn't pull him off
without a risk to her. Months later
he drowned the mongrels in the creek.

I'd have shattered glass,
sliced my arms and chest on razor wire.
For hours as a kid I hid beneath her window,
came with every movement
behind the blind, her or her sister,
hard to tell.

A good man, a family man,
I'm still tinder to her touch.
When I'm inside her, she's not there.
That doesn't stop me, though little
pleasure's in it. Like going back
to the house where you grew up
and no one's home but sadness.

Too much red-eye and I'm rough.
I need to taste what's underneath her skin.
Midday when she walks by my store
and I'm waiting on a customer,
my wife beside me, making change,
I have to dig my elbows in my ribs
to keep from crying out. She wears
my hands beneath her skirt.

Nothing I do resembles a life
if she's not in it. Some nights,
my family sound asleep in the house
that holds them brick by brick,
I walk to the river and the river takes me in.
Like an older brother it drags me under
but it will not let me drown.

HIS WIFE: NO WORD CAN HOLD IT

The wife's the last,
but I knew from the start.
As a kid I watched him
hang around the edge of things
to catch a glimpse. Across the schoolyard
his long gaze bent around my friends and me
to stroke her face. I wanted
what it was she had. No word can hold it,
now or then. A bird must feel it
in its wings, a salmon rising.

Lately I follow him, drift to the edge
of town in my white nightgown,
sometimes a neighbour's sprinkler
forgotten on the grass, its *wish, wish, wish*
wetting my feet. Most nights this is
as far as I will go – I stare across the road
like a ghost who's lost her way,
watch the curtains at her window
suck in and out as if the house itself is breathing.
So much life in her and mine in pieces.

I could make him choose,
but what's the use? He married me
and she won't have him
longer than a night.

When he slides between our sheets
near morning, he believes he keeps
her scent a secret. How can he not sense
my knowing? I curl around him,
pretending sleep, pray her smell
will soak into my skin and
he will take me hard
without the gentleness he thinks I want.

So much to see through the windshield
and on either side
you don't need to look behind.
If the car breaks down you walk,
follow deer trails through the coulees,
cow paths through pastures.
They'll lead you to a yard, perhaps
a woman who turns a handle to separate
the cream. Likely as not she'll feed you
as she did me, asking little in return.
Good with my hands I can do anything
I've a mind to, a week or more.

On the road everything changes
with the changing light. Pods of clouds
swim over fields, darkening the wheat.
From ditches wild roses drench me
with a brief and helpless longing
I thought I'd lost. Amazing what you leave
and keep on going. Near Maple Creek

a herd of antelope bunch in a circle,
a sure sign of cold coming on.
I can't help but wonder what a man
would feel in the centre, their
soft breath, those dark eyes upon him.

In one of the towns everyone's left
for the city down the road, two signs
hang above the nailed-shut doorways of the bar:
Gents, then *Ladies and Escorts*.
Once, a man could drink alone,
the wife and kids waiting in the car.

In any town that's living
you can stay in rooms above the bar.
You pay in cash, and the barkeep
leads you up the stairs – cracked linoleum,
a rust-streaked toilet down the hall.
Above the doorknob I read *Vacant*.

Wind rocks the Texaco, the Esso sign
in whatever town I'm in,
the metal hinges squeal like rats
bursting from stubble set on fire.
We used to tie our pant legs
at the ankles with binder twine.

Sleepless and cold, I look out the window
at the street below, darker than a river
in the deep of night. Sometimes a thin
poor music drifts from a house I can't see into.
Mornings I wake up with a start,
think I've left them in the car,
windows frosted, the motor running.
When I open the door I cannot wake them,
the breath I see no one's but my own.

THE OLDER SISTER: SELF-PORTRAIT

My little sister knows
my skin's no barrier
to wind, sorrow, snow,
our mother's madness.
I wish I could be bored
with things – the red of
willow, a boy's flat nipple,
the two-headed calf
our father killed
with one stroke of the maul.

There is no sadness
I can't enter. Picking
the locks with my teeth,
gnawing the thread
that holds a mind together.

My thirteenth summer
I found a wasps' nest
shaped like a head and empty.
I lived there for a month
with my sting,
made strips of paper,
mixing with my spit
slivers I chewed with this
hard mouth.

*There is a
sadness
I can't
enter*

When I was thirsty
and needed company
I sipped small drops of water
from my sister's eye.

Our mother said the war made her father
strange. In the middle of the night
he'd wake up screaming. Someone had slid
a cadaver's leg between the bedclothes.
A gruesome thing, white and cold,
he'd throw it from the mattress,
him landing with it on the floor.

No convincing him the leg was his.
He pounded it in rage, tried to tear it from
his body. Our grandmother's pity turned
to shame. The neighbours seemed to hush
when she came near. His flying out of bed
a joke they passed from mouth to mouth:
her tongue's so sharp, her smell's that bad,
a snapping turtle nests there in her thatch.

Our mother said it came as a relief
when he weakened with TB,
fear shifting to his lungs. Perhaps
the right one had been ripped
from a soldier gassed at Ypres,
then stitched into his own pale chest.
At least our grandmother couldn't
doubt what she had seen
when she took the four-hour train trip
to Fort San, patients wheeled

to screened verandahs in their beds,
his with metal bars on either side,
the cage of an animal, half-tamed.

In spite of risk she smuggled
one of his hankies home,
showed anyone who'd look
this certificate of blood
to prove him sane.

THEIR MOTHER: STRUCK BY LIGHTNING

Struck by lightning as a girl
I got up and walked away,
a white horse dead beside me
in the field, a burned smell
all around as if I'd passed
a chicken through a flame
to singe the feathers from its skin.

Maybe that's what made me
strange, that silver blade
hammered to a thinness
that had no heft, piercing
my left side. My hair
stood straight on end
just before the thunder's
boom, someone held me
by my braids
then dropped me
to the ground. The water
broke above. Hours later
when I fell through the door
my mother thought I'd drowned.

I felt only a tingling
in the fingers of one hand
till my husband drove away,
our daughters crying

and tugging on my sleeve
to pull me from the window.
It was a stormy season,
shingles flew from the house
like wooden crows,
one night a bolt struck
the lightning rod, a mourning
dove exploded from the roof.

The half of me that once held light
ran with pins and needles
stitching fire. The other side
went dark. I couldn't see
from my right eye.
Soon nothing happened
that was right.

My parents found no carcass,
no blackened patch of grass,
no proof I hadn't lied.
The horse must've up
and run away half-stunned,
white mane crackling.
Or lighter than a girl
the bolt straddling his back
rode him deep into the ground.

THE MOTHER: WITHOUT BLESSING

One daughter's too good for me,
the other a whore. A married man
rolls in her stink. It's my house
they rut in, thinking I can't hear.
She used to care for me,
the spitting image, some would say.
When I cry out she threatens
to gag me in my bed.

The younger one won't visit
with her husband.
Sends us junk as if
we're worth as little.
Rugs braided from rags,
a piece of jewellery
that cheapens the skin.
I don't remember much
of them as children.

There was a man,
a satin dress
I can't get into.
It's there on the wall,
my face half-veiled, a funny
hat on my head.
How can so much happen
then be gone?

Once, I spoke in tongues.
Now words dissolve
like wafers in my mouth,
bland and thin,
without blessing.

THE OLDER SISTER: GRANDMOTHER'S BEDROOM

Behind the mahogany door
we fingered the chenille spread,
its tufts like buds that never opened,
yellow roses eaten from the inside out.
If you lay there barelegged a summer
afternoon when you awoke
swirls of nubs intaglioed your skin.
She thought reading was a sin and never
baked on Sundays. On the walls
the photographs were oval,
never square, the glass curved
like the ground lens of a telescope
staring at the opposite of space.
The small spool bed a family heirloom,
we couldn't believe she'd slept there
with a man or that she'd birthed
her babies between its twisting posts.
There were our mother's stories about Grandad,
the leg he'd turned from flesh to wood.
Could we believe her? We didn't want to know.
Whatever secrets Grandma held, she wound
in tissue like bits of worn lace too precious
for our touch. The last day we saw her
I pincurled her hair. It took no time at all
to twist each strand, cotton fluff without the seed.
Her scalp pink as baby mice beneath my fingers

frightened me, and the smell that rose
from her old woman's lap
like something she'd forgotten
to throw out.

THE YOUNGER SISTER: TO HEAL THE PAST

Younger, no matter what my age,
I'm the ordinary one, temperate
as a Coastal winter, merely rain
in its abundance, my husband and I
my only family here. Clematis
climbs our neighbour's trellis to the sky
like a prayer made out of flowers.
On the shortest day verbena's
musty fragrance soaks the air.

Twice weekly at the school
I lead pupils through their ABC's,
insisting they sing *zed* not *zee*.
All day I hold the pleasure
of watching someone's child
push a pencil through the curve
and bar of a crooked **e**. I'd forgotten
how difficult it is to make a letter.

My only child's grown up. He never
knew my mother or the violent
storms that roll across the prairies.
Here I'm no one's daughter,
no one's sister. Just a teacher's aid,
a baker, if I do say so myself,
of some renown. Folks stop by
for angel cakes made from scratch,

the yolks turned into jelly rolls
that rise only slightly in the pan.

Unlike my neighbour whose preserves
win ribbons at the Saanich fair,
I don't can. Nothing should outlast
its season – my sister, wild with grace,
my mother in her satin dress,
a gloved hand resting on my father's forearm.

"Branches bend with fruit this hot July,"
I write my sister, as if she wanted
the weather and its anecdotes,
its spells to pin inside an almanac
to heal the past. Nothing goes to waste:
yellow plums fall half-eaten
by the crows, the resident raccoons,
who ripen any fruit they find
warming it between
their small black hands.

Crow, what treasures you bring me.
Something made of bones and feathers,
something blind. One of the boys
who followed me as a child
comes to me at night, his rightful wife
drugged by his desire. He roots in me
for something he won't find,
his hands on either side of my head
so I must look at him and cannot drift away.
Though I'm sick to death of beauty
he says, *Look in my eyes.*
See how fine you are.

After a night of him and whisky, I walk
into light's brass fist, its knuckles
gleaming. My cheek splits and darkens,
my nose bleeds. Now my mother's
still and quiet as if I've strapped her
to the mattress the way a farmer tries
to rope the wind, chain it to a windmill
to keep it from his rows of seed.
Days I lived inside her.
No one has the right to pull you
through her eyes.

In me a man's been everywhere
a man can go. Not my father.

He gentled me. *Say fox,*
he said. My eyes turned green.
I can't remember what I knew –
it was larger than any telling
like the heron's story, like the heart's.
I tended her. So many years
I swore I'd leave, marry someone
who wouldn't stay. Still
I wear our mother's cotton,
her gabardine, the loose folds of her skin.
No one's burden but my own.

Everything yearns –
that stone in your hand,
that singular blade of grass.
Don't think it's only for the light.

3

Walking into the Future

FROM GOLDEN AND THE RIVER

At daybreak he left Golden and the river
dropping into the canyon. A mountain range
to cross and then the foothills,
the long, unrolling plains before the valley
and linked lakes of Qu'Appelle.

That morning I didn't know
where he'd started from or when
but I felt something different on my skin
as I walked the shore of Echo Lake –
the wake of his car in the wind 800 miles away
stirred the air around me.

Later he'd tell me his last night in B.C.
he'd slept with a woman who wanted him
to stay. She lent him 100 bucks for gas,
not knowing I was waiting where the money
would run out. Bad as me and crazy, he'd say
the damnedest things and I'd want his mouth.
I didn't know he'd last longer than a life.

That summer "It's a Heartache" blared
from every radio. I could see him in the car
caught inside the song, the greedy gut of heat,
fingers drumming the wheel, black T-shirt
wet with sweat, pulled tight across his chest.
The button on his jeans could burn a finger.

I couldn't sit still. I watched the sun
sink behind where I guessed he'd be,
the lake an afterglow. On the wooden walk
I paced beneath the cottonwood
where wind was loudest, in the leaves
a thousand voices miraculous with longing.

When the tree went quiet I climbed the hill.
Washed in starlight I watched his car
cleave the night, leaving everything that wasn't me
behind him, the river out of Golden
a darkness now, falling blindly to the sea.

WATCHING MY LOVER

I watch him hold his mother
as she vomits into a bowl.
After, he washes her face
with a wet cloth and we try
to remove her soiled gown
tied in the back with strings.

Unable to lift her
I pull the green cotton
from under the blankets, afraid
I'll tear her skin.
He removes the paper diaper.
No one has taught us
how to do this, what to say.
Everything's so fragile here
a breath could break you.

She covers her breasts with hands
bruised from tubes and needles,
turns her face away.
It's okay, Mom, he says.
*Don't feel shy. I've undressed
dozens of women in my time.*
In this room where my lover
bares his mother, we three laugh.

Later, I curl naked beside him
in our bed, listen to his sleeping,
breath by breath. So worn out
he burns with fever – the fires
his flesh lights to keep him
from the cold.

Though he has washed
I smell her on his skin
as if she has licked him
from head to toe
with her old woman's tongue
so everyone who lies with him
will know he's still
his mother's son.

LETTER FROM THE RETREAT OF ST. SCHOLASTICA

The aches in my legs have begun again,
the pain so wide I feel it in my stomach
and not the source, as if that could be
pinned like a moth to a board, identified –
Antheraea Polyphemus. I told you
I would write when it came back.

A black cat visits every morning
for the little milk I give her,
fur dotted with the eggs of lice.
I could leave a bowl of scraps
but then she'd give up hunting
and the monks won't feed her when I'm gone.
Most of them grew up on farms, believe
an animal should work or be eaten.

Yesterday a finch flew up from the canola,
then another and another like lights coming on.
Such beauty here, my love. I need it
just a little longer.

The sky's blue brings the ocean and you
nearer than you are. Remember Sidney Spit,
the sun hot, both of us one body gleaming,
no one on the beach for miles
till a little girl marched by us with a bucket
then walked past again.

We didn't know if she had seen or not.
Next morning I found sand in our bed
as if left there by a dream.

I stroke the cat anyway and talk to her.
Will I be here when the eggs break open?
Funny what we use to measure time.
The nights so long without you I imagine
death is sleeplessness, not the peace
we've been promised. Soon I'll be ready
to come home.

I want to offer you my breasts, whole
and perfect as St. Agatha's glowing on a platter.
In the paintings they look like peach halves,
round side up and flushed with ripeness.
Others see them differently. Here I've learned
she is the patron saint of artisans who fashion bells
from bronze, hands and faces gold above the vats,
and on her feast day the churches serve
round loaves of bread.

At dusk I remove my glasses as you taught me.
Between the leaden boughs of spruce
the sky breaks into pieces more beautiful
than the glass at Chartres, those ancient
fragments of rare blue,
what the naked eye half-blind can see!
Where I am, every hour, the bells are ringing.

ADVICE FOR THE SOUL

1.
Choose a stone.
Preferably a limestone
from the Tyndall Quarry.
Curl inside the fossil
of a nautilus. It has more
chambers than the heart.

2.
A chameleon's
your best companion
changing colours as it moves
as you change shape and size,
how much of you is darkness,
how much of you is light.

3.
You may find yourself
invisible to any eye
no matter what your pyrotechnics,
the beauty of your carapace
or feathered throat – the yellow
of meadowlark's you'd be
so warm there, you'd sail
the wheat fields on its song.

4.
Consider prairie brome.
Short and unassuming
yet its roots dream furlongs
beneath the earth.

5.
Move inside the white
spot of a fawn, the one
above its left front hoof.

This will be most auspicious,
an opportunity to improve
your delicacy and grace
when you leap from wing to whisker
to the baleen of a whale,
the nipple of a nursing bear.

6.
Look for something made of iron.
Search for seams of salt,
water pools in fissures,
a thing that changes
by standing still.

7.
Slip inside the rat's gut.
Kind mother to her babies,
untiring forager of seed,
leaf and flesh.

When the ship is sinking
first creature of the kingdom
in the new-found land.

SUMMER'S END, SASKATCHEWAN

Swaths of wheat cross the fields
in currents so thick they cannot move.
Summer run-off. How much ripeness
they must carry, how much light
caught in stalk and seed head.
I want to float down their clotted water,
my body's sails catching the heart's
held breath. It takes me nowhere,
this slow flux, the rows stopped
in mid-motion, the day's long lethargy.
Wind minnows flicker in streams of wheat,
in the lingering of an eye, golden
like the goat's at the edge of the field
where the grass isn't cut. His horizontal pupils
slant the light, making everything lie down.

WALKING INTO THE FUTURE

Months after, your mother's death is
something you pull on every morning,
old flannel tight across your chest.
It's been a hard year – your drinking, stopping,
stopping again, and I've been on the road
too much. Learned a distance I didn't know
before, a space that separates one
phone call, one city from the next. Still
everything continues, including love,
including loneliness. It's the same
house we live in. The same tree
stains our deck with yellow plums
predictable in late July. Wasps feast
on this sweet mating with the sun.
What changes? Lately there are things
I do not tell you – I ache inside, you
sadden me. Away too long I carry
my bags up the four steps to our porch,
hesitate, as I've never done before.
Sun-blind, I walk into the future,
see only shapes – a couch, a chair,
and someone rising. I don't know who
you will be.

WHAT YOU REMEMBER REMAINS

The cockatoo named Joey wears
my father's hooded eyes, his look
of dumb surprise at dying. *Kiss me*,
Joey says, which isn't what he means.
It's cockatoo for *feed me* or, better yet,
my father small and turning yellow
in his bed, cockatoo for *set me free*.

Our new cat glides through the door
on your mother's legs, long and white.
In a wicker basket on my desk
she crosses her slim ankles
and seems as vain, your mother
hitching up her skirt when she thought
no one could see, the lace of her slip
lisping above her knees.

Yesterday a crow strode across the grass
with my Welsh Grandpa's stiffness
as if the bird had ruined his knees
from sixty years of gardening. Now
I put out jam on scraps of bread
and bother him with roses,
ask why the buds won't open,
how much bone they need to grow.

Kiss me – at least we know
what it means and who is speaking.
Sometimes late at night they come to us
with what they carry from the past,
that look, that way of walking,
that softness around the mouth
where grief begins.

THE OTHER WOMAN

Nearly twenty years ago and finally
I can think of her. She used to dial,
put the older of the two boys on the line.
Only four, *Daddy*, he'd say,
when are you coming home? till his father
clicked the receiver down. He'd left them
$10,000 and a yellow truck, came to me
with more than his pockets empty.

We struck out across the prairies,
wind roaring through the car, the road
hurtling us into the sky like a midway ride.
Every night a bottle of wine, a cheap motel,
we went so far we came back animal
and wild. No child could hold us.

The first time he visited his sons
she wore clothes he'd never seen before,
hair shampooed and newly permed.
Stay the night, she said, *save the price of a room.*
Home with me his hands stammered
down my belly in a language they'd forgotten,
one with several words for guilt and pain.
I almost lost him then.

Now it's she who phones
late at night, the boys grown up.

When I answer, she doesn't ask for him.
There's a silence, both of us breathing,
and I think of her mouth almost touching
the phone – as close as we have come.
Sometimes the next morning I keep quiet.
In twenty years I've never seen her face.

Nineteen seventy-eight, the end of summer
is a snapshot I never took –
the first time I see him with the boys.
In Okanagan Lake he holds around the waist
his younger son, pale legs kicking.
So beautiful together, it's an ache
I've carried since, something small and shining.
A stranger, from the shore I observe
the other boy thrash towards the raft.
She may be standing in the trees, invisible,
watching. She should have been.

If the child had been drowning,
if his father had turned to me
and the little one, free,
kicked into deeper water,
I couldn't have moved,
couldn't have saved them,
so fierce I was
holding on to my new life.

A KIND OF LOVE

You can see it
in my graduation photograph.
You're Daddy's little girl, he said,
his arm heavy around my shoulders,
his face too naked, a sloppy
smile sliding to one side.
I held him up. Mom tied his shoes.
His love made me ashamed.

Some days I felt protective,
his hangdog look at breakfast
when no one talked to him but me,
sugar spilling from his spoon.
Don't tell Mum, he'd say
on Sundays when he took me boating,
sunk his third empty in the lake.
At home, she fried a chicken
in case he didn't catch a fish,
waited and kept things warm.
Even so, he died too soon.

Now I wait for you as if
you've spent a summer afternoon
in waves of wind and sunlight. I know
you've hidden a bottle somewhere
upstairs in your room. So far

I've stopped myself from looking
though I can't find what to do.

More and more I'm Daddy's
little girl in peau de soi,
my first long dress, its false
sheen a wash of mauve.
When you lean into me
the same look's on your face
as in the photograph,
your smile's undone.

Among the other things
it could be named
this too is love, the kind
I'm most familiar with –
the weight I claim
I cannot bear and do,
and do.

Through the porch window
we watched them dance – our friends'
teenage daughter and your son,
twenty-one this year and with us for a visit.
They didn't hear our knock,
music so loud my chest bone shuddered,
the soles of my feet hummed.

He bobbed and swayed, golden with sweat
and lamplight. Legs wrapped around his waist
she hugged his naked chest, secure in the grace
that held her, her prettiness against his flesh
suddenly a fragile, dangerous beauty.

Next to our deaths, the hardest thing
to imagine is our parents making love. Now
the age we are, surely it's our children,
faces radiant with lust. The sheen of sex
on limbs bathed and cradled, that smell
trailing from their shoulders its cape of musk.
We don't want to hear them when they come.

Later in the car alone with him
you asked, *What's wrong with you,
she's far too young*, then repeated
your father's words from years ago,
your girlfriend three months' pregnant.

Barely sixteen you wanted more from him,
something that could save you,
turn you back. All he had to offer
was a father's rage and fear.
Is your brain between your legs?

You should have answered yes,
the brain is everywhere.
Some days my cunt's an existentialist.
When I touch your anus
my fingers ponder the origin of stars.

Can your son imagine us as we are now?
My brain's beneath your tongue
moving as it moves from mouth
to breast to earlobe as your cock,
so cerebral in the candlelight,
thinks its way inside me.

AFTER READING *THE GREAT FIRES*

The sorrow of the old male poet,
a pure and solipsistic singing,
what comes close to happiness
a foreign tongue, a hut without a wife,
a rope pulled hand over hand, the clear
water of the spirit carried to the mouth
made rusty by what holds it.

Last night I held a baby to my breast,
my nipple aching when I woke.
So many years without a child
I thought that need excised
but everything returns, the healing
stretched delicate as skin that covers
where the bones don't join.

On the couch, cat on my lap,
his back balancing the book I read,
he lifts his eyes, gazes above my head.
We hear a thin, high squealing.
It's too much for the cat and me.
Rats tunnel through the insulation,
giving birth. Inside these living walls
the house at night's exquisite, its candles
and its rugs, my body sweet in its decay.

Lately the cat wants to sleep
under the covers, curl against my belly
but my lover finds it strange. At night
I lie in his arms, thinking of the old poet,
his sadness and his tales of decadence,
the small silver instruments
used on a woman who loves the pain
that can be stopped
or started with one word.

A live trap. You've placed it by the pond,
baited it with what the experts say
raccoons will eat – one egg, grape jelly
gleaming on a slice of bread.
So far you've caught a squirrel
and our neighbour's ginger tabby
who loves to dip his paw above the fish.
I don't ask if you've been drinking.

The usual talk about the weather –
stormy here but there, a heat wave.
Back to the cat, then the shubunkin.
You haven't seen him since the raccoon
upset the lily pots and ate the water hyacinth.
This afternoon you'll have to strip, wade
into the pool like someone being baptised.
Born again you'll put things right,
a summer of good intentions – I won't ask.

Last night you and the raccoon, eyes red
and fierce with moonlight, came face
to face. You threw a stone and missed
though you were close enough
to grab his tail. Every evening,
you tell me, before you go to bed
you look inside the darkness;
if it's empty – as it usually is –
you replace the egg.

SPILT MILK

i.
Spilt milk in the middle of the floor
on red linoleum. Island View Dairy,

a small white pool. Onanistic.
Don't cry over it. Your mother

three months dead. Even at the end
she sat up in bed to carmine her lips.

Hand unsteady, her mouth grew larger,
said less. A red-rimmed darkness, breathing.

Fall in the orchards and suddenly you're back
in your attic room, the smells of childhood.

From the apples, wasps move in
so thick and slow they're beams

of sunlight brightening your skin,
the penis you hold in your hand.

You think your mother doesn't know.
She is pressing shirts in the room beneath you.

You can hear the stutter of buttons
under the iron, the steam sighing.

Hovering above you the wasps gleam
calm and quiet yet you've seen them

eat a hole through the heart
of a butchered pig.

You like the danger of them —
close but never touching,

your mother wiping her forehead in the heat,
thin milk spilling down your hand.

ii.
This morning two pileated woodpeckers
renovate the maple, punch a skylight

through the branches, knock down a wall
so the sun pours through.

Such noisy workers yet you don't
hear them. What are you listening to?

There's been too much grief for us,
dead wood, sow bugs eating the orchid,

the one called moth. Its petals
the texture of grafted skin.

You tell me our friend has seen
a shadow on his lung. The X-ray

ern Bergamot, Larkspur,
ntian near the Manitoba border,
ers in the Cypress Hills.
names out loud,
fter page as if the past were
with whom I've made a pact.
rimrose, Yarrow, Wild Flax –
ld Sorrow look like, what fruit
ear? I have in mind no colour.
d, or blue it would bloom
undance this July, its flowers
a fragrant heaviness,
ny fingers its leaves softly
e fine hairs of a lover's wrist.
ed the sepals with my tongue
ise and then repeat it, an aftertaste,
time. Wild near the marsh
nd of Rue where only yesterday
potted frogs leapt in imitation
art's strange fondness
is lost.

a window into the sunken gardens
of his flesh, the dark blossoms.

He knows the fine art, ikebana.
Now he must learn the body's

formal arrangements. Contorted willow
and the perfect stone, a lichen scrawl.

Goodness and mercy, all we can say.
On the phone his voice

businesslike, precise – in the morning
he coughs webs of blood.

That flash of red is what you see
before you know

it's a woodpecker causing
all the racket. Wake up, wake up.

Work to be done
and winter's coming on.

iii.
The moon's a hip bone at rest in its socket.
It turns, and night takes one giant stride

across the earth. Nothing is lost.
Stars pick out the hundred shapes of cats.

The cold centre of November, the brightest
colour is remembrance red.

What do the dead recall under the stones,
the tangle of roots or kelp,

the glass frames on the mantel?
Do they know us any more?

The weight of a spoon in the fingers,
a shovel's handshake with the earth,

a blue-white pool on the kitchen floor?
Don't cry. The cat will lap it up.

Snow's opposite, my father's ashes
fell from my palm to the lake.

You were trying to recite
the 23rd Psalm, my mother's request.

Goodness and mercy, all you could say,
your voice breaking. Take one step back

into the world, the shadows memory casts
across the mind, the mutable lung,

your childhood wasps wintering
inside you, their lazy buzz

the beginning of every song
your mother sang to make you sleep.

He is the dog who leads
the blind, tows their shadows
towards the light,
their soft feet hesitant
and bruised

their faces
when they look at you
so naked and guileless

you wonder what it is
those dead eyes see:
ash tree, lesser crow,
black dog, black water?

Sometimes he is a boat
drifting through the dark
with his heavy human cargo,
leading them towards what shines.

Wild
Close
Wind
I read
flip pa
a bota
Eveni
what w
would
Yellow
in rich
a burd
betwee
furred.
If I tou
I'd say
a hint
I find a
leopar
of the
for wha

ACKNOWLEDGEMENTS

Some of the poems in this book have appeared in the following magazines: *Descant, Event, Canadian Forum, Carousel, CVII, Grain, Dandelion, Room of One's Own, The Southern Review, The New Quarterly, Nimrod, Washington Square,* and *Poetry Africa '97.* Four of the poems were part of a chapbook called *The Transparency of Grief,* the winner of the 2nd Annual {m}Öthêr Tøñgué Press Poetry Chapbook Contest and published by the press in 1996.

Harold Rhenisch's wonderful poem "The Night of My Conception" inspired my two poems that borrow his title. The line "a shovel's handshake with the earth" in the poem "Spilt Milk" is a variation of a metaphor from Kevin Paul's "Still Falling."

These poems owe much to the encouragement, love, and advice of my companion, Patrick Lane, and to the editing skills of the demanding Donna Bennett and the sharp-eyed Heather Sangster. In addition, my friends Jan Zwicky and Jane Southwell Munro shared their insightful reactions to many of the poems. I'd like to thank the Saskatchewan Artists/Writers' Colony for providing me with a writing home, and the University of Victoria for a travel grant and the study leave that allowed me to polish this manuscript. Thanks also to the Canada Council.